WHAT WOULD YOU RATHER DO?

PAPERMD
Kids

Thank you for choosing our book!

We do our best to provide you with a high-quality product. However, mistakes always can happen. If you find any issue with our book, let us now at

papermoodbooks@gmail.com

We will make sure you get a brand new copy of the book right away!.

We are still developing and enhancing our products. Your opinion means the world for us!

Please, support us and leave a review on our Amazon page! This will help us a lot.

CONTENTS

- Contents
- How to play
- Level 1
- Level 2
- Level 3
- Level 4
- Level 5
- Level 6
- Level 7

HOW TO PLAY?

Are you ready for a lot of laughs and even more challenges?

During this game, you will need to make funny, gross, and hard choices! Be prepared!

- Gather all your favourite ones: your friends, your siblings, your parents! The more people involved in the game, the more laughter there will be!

- Choose a judge! Flip a coin and decide who will be the judge for the first question. The judge should be changed after every question. You can go clockwise or let the person who won the last question be the judge for the next one. This rule is up to you!

- The judge reads the question and lets the others answer.

- Now, it's your time to answer and explain your choice! Be imaginative!

The judge chooses the more creative, reasonable, or funny explanation and gives this person a point. In case there are only two people playing, the judge gives a point ranges from 1-5 (5 points for the best answer).

The winner's name and point score should be written in the box below the question.

The game is divided into seven levels. At each level, you will find questions with different complexity. When all players answer all questions in level, the points should be summed up.

A person with the biggest amount of points wins the level!

In case of a tie, there is an additional question provided at the end of each level. Ask this question and let the group vote for the best answer!

Good luck and have fun!

WHAT WOULD YOU RATHER DO?

LEVEL

1

WOULD YOU RATHER

live where it rains all day

OR

snowing all the time?

WINNER: POINTS:

WOULD YOU RATHER

have 13 siblings

OR

no siblings?

WINNER: POINTS:

LEVEL 1

WOULD YOU RATHER

run as fast as a cheetah

OR

swim as fast as a dolphin?

WINNER: POINTS:

WOULD YOU RATHER

have a dog who speaks

OR

a dog who cooks you
meals?

WINNER: POINTS:

LEVEL 1

WOULD YOU RATHER

meet your favourite singer

OR

your favourite actor?

WINNER: POINTS:

WOULD YOU RATHER

eat french fries for every
meal

OR

eat rice for every meal?

WINNER: POINTS:

WOULD YOU RATHER

train a dog to dance ballet

OR

train a elephant to ride a
bike?

WINNER: POINTS:

WOULD YOU RATHER

be in room full of dirty
people

OR

in a room full of stinky
people?

WINNER: POINTS:

WOULD YOU RATHER

never eat chocolate again

OR

chips?

WINNER: POINTS:

WOULD YOU RATHER

skydive into enormous
bowl of jelly beans

OR

dive in a chocolate
pudding?

WINNER: POINTS:

LEVEL 1

WOULD YOU RATHER

have to eat 30 peach pits

OR

all the seeds from 30
apples?

WINNER: POINTS:

WOULD YOU RATHER

live underground

OR

underwater for all your
life?

WINNER: POINTS:

LEVEL 1

WOULD YOU RATHER

live in a place where
always is freezing cold

OR

burning hot?

WINNER: POINTS:

WOULD YOU RATHER

eat a hair soup

OR

a sandwich with earwax
paste?

WINNER: POINTS:

LEVEL 1

WOULD YOU RATHER

be able to teleport

OR

be able to be invisible?

WINNER: POINTS:

WOULD YOU RATHER

eat a live fish

OR

a dead bird?

WINNER: POINTS:

LEVEL 1

WOULD YOU RATHER

drink a glass of really spicy
chilli sauce

OR

eat a sandwitch found in a
garbage can?

WINNER: POINTS:

WOULD YOU RATHER

have 10 brothers

OR

have 10 sisters?

WINNER: POINTS:

LEVEL 1

WOULD YOU RATHER

have only 8 fingers

OR

only 3 toes?

WINNER: POINTS:

WOULD YOU RATHER

have a unicorn horn

OR

burp uncontrollably?

WINNER: POINTS:

LEVEL 1

COUNT THE POINTS!

NAME	POINTS

BONUS!

WOULD YOU RATHER

roll around in the sand

OR

roll around in wet clay?

WINNER of 1st LEVEL:

IN CASE OF TIE, USE THE BONUS QUESTION!

LEVEL 1

WHAT WOULD YOU RATHER DO?

LEVEL

2

WOULD YOU RATHER

have permanently pointy
teeth

OR

have permanently tangled
hair?

WINNER: POINTS:

WOULD YOU RATHER

be trapped in the room
with 2 large spiders

OR

100 small mosquitoes?

WINNER: POINTS:

LEVEL 2

WOULD YOU RATHER

spend a night in an
amusement park

OR

on the beach party?

WINNER: POINTS:

WOULD YOU RATHER

have to poop 10 times a
day

OR

be able to pee only once a
day?

WINNER: POINTS:

WOULD YOU RATHER

be a wizard

OR

be a superhero?

WINNER: POINTS:

WOULD YOU RATHER

peel potatoes with your
teeth

OR

wash the dishes with your
tongue?

WINNER: POINTS:

LEVEL 2

WOULD YOU RATHER

have the nose of a dog

OR

the eyes of a cat?

WINNER: POINTS:

WOULD YOU RATHER

wear underwear one size
too small

OR

shoes two sizes too big?

WINNER: POINTS:

WOULD YOU RATHER

have nightmares once a
week

OR

find a dead body?

WINNER: POINTS:

WOULD YOU RATHER

dance like a monkey

OR

dance like a bear?

WINNER: POINTS:

LEVEL 2

WOULD YOU RATHER

always be the smallest

OR

the thinner person in the room?

WINNER: POINTS:

WOULD YOU RATHER

have 20 dogs

OR

30 cats?

WINNER: POINTS:

WOULD YOU RATHER

have to use a public toilet
when you've got diarrhea

OR

have someone with
diarrhea use your toilet?

WINNER: POINTS:

WOULD YOU RATHER

bathe in saltwater

OR

bathe in hand sanitizer?

WINNER: POINTS:

WOULD YOU RATHER

wake up on the desert
island alone

OR

with your worst enemy?

WINNER: POINTS:

WOULD YOU RATHER

eat spaghetti with a spoon

OR

eat pizza with chopsticks?

WINNER: POINTS:

WOULD YOU RATHER

have no teeth

OR

have no hair?

WINNER: POINTS:

WOULD YOU RATHER

encounter dinosaurs

OR

aliens?

WINNER: POINTS:

LEVEL 2

WOULD YOU RATHER

never have to go to school

OR

never have any friends?

WINNER: POINTS:

WOULD YOU RATHER

swallow a worm

OR

suck on a worm?

WINNER: POINTS:

LEVEL 2

COUNT THE POINTS!

NAME	POINTS

BONUS!

WOULD YOU RATHER

eat off a cat plate

OR

eat off a used dog plate?

WINNER of 2nd LEVEL:

IN CASE OF TIE, USE THE BONUS QUESTION!

WHAT WOULD YOU RATHER DO?

LEVEL

3

WOULD YOU RATHER

have someone sneeze in
your face

OR

blow their nose into your
outfit?

WINNER: POINTS:

WOULD YOU RATHER

get tickled for five minutes

OR

have to touch a tarantula
for one minute?

WINNER: POINTS:

WOULD YOU RATHER

eat spaghetti through a
straw

OR

blended into a smoothie?

WINNER: POINTS:

WOULD YOU RATHER

smell like dog's poop

OR

smell like old lady's
perfumes?

WINNER: POINTS:

LEVEL 3

WOULD YOU RATHER

be stuck on an island
alone

OR

with someone who farts a
lot?

WINNER: POINTS:

WOULD YOU RATHER

be the youngest

OR

the oldest sibling?

WINNER: POINTS:

WOULD YOU RATHER

use only dog shampoo

OR

smell like a dog?

WINNER: POINTS:

WOULD YOU RATHER

have unlimited donuts

OR

ice creams?

WINNER: POINTS:

LEVEL 3

WOULD YOU RATHER

have to announce to
everyone when you're
about to fart

OR

when you're about to pee?

WINNER: POINTS:

WOULD YOU RATHER

wear winter clothes in
summer

OR

summer clothes in winter?

WINNER: POINTS:

WOULD YOU RATHER

get a pie smashed in your
face

OR

smash a pie in your
friend's face?

WINNER: POINTS:

WOULD YOU RATHER

drink stinky water every
day

OR

eat untasty food every
day?

WINNER: POINTS:

LEVEL 3

WOULD YOU RATHER

find out someone spat in
your food

OR

someone spat in your
water?

WINNER: POINTS:

WOULD YOU RATHER

pour poison on your hands

OR

pour acid on your feet?

WINNER: POINTS:

LEVEL 3

WOULD YOU RATHER

make funny sounds all of
the time

OR

have to repeat everything
you say?

WINNER: POINTS:

WOULD YOU RATHER

have hairy feet

OR

hairy hands?

WINNER: POINTS:

LEVEL 3

WOULD YOU RATHER

smell like onions

OR

garlic for the rest of your life?

WINNER: POINTS:

WOULD YOU RATHER

not be able to walk but jump

OR

not be able to speak but sing?

WINNER: POINTS:

WOULD YOU RATHER

only eat foods that look
disgusting

OR

smell disgusting?

WINNER: POINTS:

WOULD YOU RATHER

pee when you cry

OR

pee when you laugh?

WINNER: POINTS:

LEVEL 3

COUNT THE POINTS!

NAME	POINTS

BONUS!

WOULD YOU RATHER

sleep in a very small,
bright room

OR

in a very big, empty and
dark room?

WINNER of 3rdLEVEL:

IN CASE OF TIE, USE THE BONUS QUESTION!

WHAT WOULD YOU RATHER DO?

LEVEL

4

WOULD YOU RATHER

lick a toilet seat

OR

lick a toilet floor?

WINNER: POINTS:

WOULD YOU RATHER

give a kiss to your dog

OR

your grandma kiss you in
front of your friends?

WINNER: POINTS:

LEVEL 4

WOULD YOU RATHER

poop in your hands

OR

poop in your friend's
hands?

WINNER: POINTS:

WOULD YOU RATHER

dress only in green clothes

OR

wear only dresses and
skirts?

WINNER: POINTS:

LEVEL 4

WOULD YOU RATHER

have fingers on your feet

OR

have eyes on your belly?

WINNER: POINTS:

WOULD YOU RATHER

have fingers as long as
your hair

OR

your legs as long as your
arms?

WINNER: POINTS:

WOULD YOU RATHER

have a mustard instead of
snot in your nose

OR

have a song playing while
you fart?

WINNER: POINTS:

WOULD YOU RATHER

have an extra leg

OR

an extra hand?

WINNER: POINTS:

WOULD YOU RATHER

meet a superhero

OR

your future self?

WINNER: POINTS:

WOULD YOU RATHER

have a pet panda

OR

pet zebra?

WINNER: POINTS:

LEVEL 4

WOULD YOU RATHER

be as high as giraffe

OR

as small as a mouse?

WINNER: POINTS:

WOULD YOU RATHER

receive a gift you don't like

OR

give someone a gift and
they don't like it?

WINNER: POINTS:

LEVEL 4

WOULD YOU RATHER

sniff a dog's butt

OR

sniff a cat's butt?

WINNER: POINTS:

WOULD YOU RATHER

never cut your hair

OR

never cut your nails?

WINNER: POINTS:

LEVEL 4

WOULD YOU RATHER

eat a rotten apple

OR

eat a stale burger?

WINNER: POINTS:

WOULD YOU RATHER

drink a tea from a dirty
fish tank

OR

drink a fruit smoothie with
a few spider webs mixed
into it?

WINNER: POINTS:

LEVEL 4

WOULD YOU RATHER

eat a dead cockroach

OR

take a bath in camels
vomits?

WINNER: POINTS:

WOULD YOU RATHER

be the first person to live
on Mars

OR

have your own spaceship?

WINNER: POINTS:

LEVEL 4

WOULD YOU RATHER

have no ears

OR

no eyes?

WINNER: POINTS:

WOULD YOU RATHER

eat jam flavored poo

OR

poo-flavored peanut
butter?

WINNER: POINTS:

COUNT THE POINTS!

NAME	POINTS

BONUS!

WOULD YOU RATHER

smell like onions

OR

have to eat onions every
day?

WINNER of 4th LFVEL:

**IN CASE OF TIE, USE THE
BONUS QUESTION!**

LEVEL 4

WHAT WOULD YOU RATHER DO?

LEVEL

5

WOULD YOU RATHER

spend one month of holidays in a tent on the beach

OR

one week in a luxury hotel?

WINNER: POINTS:

WOULD YOU RATHER

have no bed

OR

no table and chairs in your house?

WINNER: POINTS:

LEVEL 5

WOULD YOU RATHER

always eat fruits and
vegetables using axe

OR

drink everything using a
small spoon?

WINNER: POINTS:

WOULD YOU RATHER

pay 10$

OR

lick a rotten fish?

WINNER: POINTS:

WOULD YOU RATHER

have a bath of spiders

OR

a shower of slugs?

WINNER: POINTS:

WOULD YOU RATHER

have ability of a
chameleon to adjust your
color to the surrounding

OR

have a shell to hide in like
a turtle?

WINNER: POINTS:

LEVEL 5

WOULD YOU RATHER

lie to your parents

OR

lie to your teacher?

WINNER: POINTS:

WOULD YOU RATHER

brush your teeth with
clean toilet water from
your own toilet

OR

lost your phone and never
found it?

WINNER: POINTS:

WOULD YOU RATHER

be a rich person with no
family

OR

a poor person with a lot of
family members?

WINNER: POINTS:

WOULD YOU RATHER

remove your eyelashes
one after the other

OR

remove your eyebrows
one after the other?

WINNER: POINTS:

WOULD YOU RATHER

have a room with no
windows

OR

room with big windows
and no blinds so everyone
can watch you.

WINNER: POINTS:

WOULD YOU RATHER

be a chef in a bakery/cake
shop

OR

in a pizzeria?

WINNER: POINTS:

WOULD YOU RATHER

have the power to heal

OR

the power to stop wars?

WINNER: POINTS:

WOULD YOU RATHER

be a famous chef

OR

have your private chef?

WINNER: POINTS:

WOULD YOU RATHER

swim in pudding

OR

ice cream?

WINNER: POINTS:

WOULD YOU RATHER

create a famous piece of
art

OR

invent a famous
invention?

WINNER: POINTS:

WOULD YOU RATHER

be bald

OR

very hairy?

WINNER: POINTS:

WOULD YOU RATHER

be an animal in a circus

OR

in a zoo?

WINNER: POINTS:

WOULD YOU RATHER

have salt get into your
eyes

OR

your nose?

WINNER: POINTS:

WOULD YOU RATHER

be a nurse

OR

be a doctor?

WINNER: POINTS:

COUNT THE POINTS!

NAME   POINTS

BONUS!

WOULD YOU RATHER

spend a day alone in a tent

OR

a night alone in your school?

WINNER of 5th LEVEL:

IN CASE OF TIE, USE THE BONUS QUESTION!

WHAT WOULD YOU RATHER DO?

LEVEL

6

WOULD YOU RATHER

be able to change into an
animal

OR

an adult once a day?

WINNER: POINTS:

WOULD YOU RATHER

be the smallest

OR

the biggest person or
Earth?

WINNER: POINTS:

LEVEL 6

WOULD YOU RATHER

be in a cage with 100
parrots

OR

be in a pool with 100
dolphins?

WINNER: POINTS:

WOULD YOU RATHER

eat a chunk of hair

OR

drink a glass of sweat?

WINNER: POINTS:

WOULD YOU RATHER

have a pet unicorn

OR

a pet dragon?

WINNER: POINTS:

WOULD YOU RATHER

eat only rice for the rest of
your life

OR

eat only pasta?

WINNER: POINTS:

WOULD YOU RATHER

be the fastest runner

OR

the best dancer?

WINNER: POINTS:

WOULD YOU RATHER

switch houses with your
best friend

OR

live in one house with your
friend and your both
families?

WINNER: POINTS:

WOULD YOU RATHER

eat only sweet food

OR

only salty food?

WINNER: POINTS:

WOULD YOU RATHER

always be late

OR

always be one hour
earlier?

WINNER: POINTS:

WOULD YOU RATHER

be forced to wear your
dad's clothes

OR

your mother's clothes?

WINNER: POINTS:

WOULD YOU RATHER

never brush your hair

OR

never brush your teeth
again?

WINNER: POINTS:

WOULD YOU RATHER

pooping in front of your
friends

OR

taking a shower in front of
your family?

WINNER: POINTS:

WOULD YOU RATHER

have a flying magic carpet

OR

have a Genie lamp?

WINNER: POINTS:

LEVEL 6

WOULD YOU RATHER

have no hair at all

OR

have no nails?

WINNER: POINTS:

WOULD YOU RATHER

be imprisoned in a luxury
prison for 1 year

OR

be homeless for 1 year?

WINNER: POINTS:

WOULD YOU RATHER

be able to talk to snakes

OR

to birds?

WINNER: POINTS:

WOULD YOU RATHER

be very good at writing

OR

be very good at math?

WINNER: POINTS:

WOULD YOU RATHER

not shower for a month

OR

stay in the same clothes
for a month?

WINNER: POINTS:

WOULD YOU RATHER

have your farts smell like
flowers

OR

have your nose pickings
taste like chocolate?

WINNER: POINTS:

COUNT THE POINTS!

NAME   **POINTS**

BONUS!

WOULD YOU RATHER

be an ogre

OR

a vampire?

WINNER of 6th LEVEL:

IN CASE OF A TIE, USE THE BONUS QUESTION!

WHAT WOULD YOU RATHER DO?

LEVEL
7

WOULD YOU RATHER

eat a bowl of dog's food

OR

drink cup of oil?

WINNER: POINTS:

WOULD YOU RATHER

have no access to a
computer

OR

have no access to the
internet?

WINNER: POINTS:

WOULD YOU RATHER

eat a small dessert before
dinner

OR

big dessert after dinner?

WINNER: POINTS:

WOULD YOU RATHER

cover yourself with honey

OR

ketchup?

WINNER: POINTS:

LEVEL 7

WOULD YOU RATHER

eat a pinch of sand

OR

lick a handful of stones?

WINNER: POINTS:

WOULD YOU RATHER

have one hand twice as
big as the other

OR

one eye twice as big as the
other?

WINNER: POINTS:

WOULD YOU RATHER

lick the car tire

OR

the seat of a public toilet?

WINNER: POINTS:

WOULD YOU RATHER

have only one best friend

OR

be the most popular kid in
school but with no real
friends?

WINNER: POINTS:

WOULD YOU RATHER

have pink long hair

OR

yellow eyes?

WINNER: POINTS:

WOULD YOU RATHER

have dozen of cockroaches
in your t-shirt

OR

in your pants?

WINNER: POINTS:

WOULD YOU RATHER

kiss your best friend's
armpit

OR

never eat ice creams
again?

WINNER: POINTS:

WOULD YOU RATHER

poop your pants

OR

use a dirty toilet to poop?

WINNER: POINTS:

WOULD YOU RATHER

live in a wizard's world

OR

superhero's world?

WINNER: POINTS:

WOULD YOU RATHER

have a dog

OR

a sibling?

WINNER: POINTS:

WOULD YOU RATHER

be a lion

OR

a monkey?

WINNER: POINTS:

WOULD YOU RATHER

not be able to say "yes"

OR

"no"?

WINNER: POINTS:

WOULD YOU RATHER

be able to read 5 books a
day

OR

never have to do
homework again?

WINNER: POINTS:

WOULD YOU RATHER

sleep in the barn

OR

in the cemetery?

WINNER: POINTS:

LEVEL 7

WOULD YOU RATHER

hold a scorpion

OR

a rat in your hands?

WINNER: POINTS:

WOULD YOU RATHER

touch your eyeball

OR

get tickled for 15 minutes?

WINNER: POINTS:

COUNT THE POINTS!

NAME   POINTS

BONUS!

WOULD YOU RATHER

be a cute puppy

OR

an ugly human?

WINNER of 7th LEVEL:

IN CASE OF TIE, USE THE BONUS QUESTION!

THANKS FOR PLAYING WITH US!

IF YOU ENJOYED IT, TAKE A LOOK FOR A DIFFERENT BOOKS AT

PAPERMOODKIDS

STORE AT AMAZON.COM

SCAN ME

Printed in Great Britain
by Amazon

75169126R00061